Heart Matters

Poems and meditations of Gods faithfulness and love

Sharon. A. Franklin
Sunesis Ministries Ltd

Copyright © 2019 Sharon A. Franklin

The right of Sharon A. Franklin to be identified as author of this work has been asserted by her in accordance with the Copyright, Designs, and Patents Act 1988

No part of this publication may be reproduced or transmitted in any form or by any means, electronic or mechanical, including photocopy, recording, or any information storage and retrieval system, without permission in writing from the author.

Unless otherwise indicated, scripture quotations are from the Holy Bible, New King James Version Copyright © 1982 Thomas Nelson, Inc. Used by permission.

Scripture quotations marked KJV are from the Holy Bible, King James Version.

Published by Sunesis Ministries Ltd. For more information about Sunesis Ministries Ltd, please visit:

www.stuartpattico.com

ISBN: 978-0-9956837-8-5

The views expressed in this book are solely those of the author and do not necessarily reflect the views of the publisher, and the publisher hereby disclaims any responsibility for them.

Contents

Preface	9
Christ within You	11
The Sun will shine again	12
Pains of Life	13
MORNING BREAKS	14
BE STILL and know	15
When Sickness Comes	16
LIVE. LIFE....LAUGH	17
The Peace of God	18
OVERWHELMED	19
A Mothers' Love	20
FAMILY MATTERS	21
PEACE	22
TRIALS COME TO MAKE YOU STRONGER	23
LOVE IS PATIENT	24
I HUNGER FOR YOU	25
DAMSEL ARISE	26
THE LOVE OF GOD	27
LIFE GOES ON	28
HE KNOWS IT ALL	29
It is FINISHED	31

Thank you	32
OUTSIDE THESE WALLS	34
Keep LOVING	35
STAND STRONG	36
Wait on the LORD	37
Take Time Out for Others	38
Smile on	39
When GOD GIVES	40
PRAISE HIM	41
Hang on in there	42
LORD YOU ARE	43
As the tears fall	45
BETTER DAYS ARE COMING	46
There is a Blessing awaiting YOU	47
The Secret place of God	48
Sleep ON	49
A FATHERS love	51
To whom Much is GIVEN	52
GODS LOVE	53
Your LOVE	54
HIS GRACE & PEACE	55
The Battle is His	56
What is FAILURE?	57

Till Thy Kingdom Come	58
He Who Died for You	59
Holy Spirit Seal Me	60
FRIENDSHIP	61
HEAR MY CRY	64
ON ANGEL WINGS	65
ALL I NEED	66
ONLY YOU	67
When God Is Silent	69
NEVER GIVE UP	71
IT'S NOT ABOUT ME	72
FORGIVENESS	73
WHO AM I?	74
WALK AWAY	76
GODS PEACE	77
FAILURE IS NOT THE END	78
SORRY IS HARD TO SAY	79
GOD HOLDS ME	80
SO MISUNDERSTOOD	81
HE SAVES HE KEEPS	82
STAY IN HIS PRESENCE	83
BLAZE ON	85
SEEK GOD FIRST	86

Come Lord Jesus...Come	87
Love Is a Curious Thing	89
Tears	91
Peace	92
Hope	93
I'm Tired	94
Enlarge my Territory	96
MORE LIKE JESUS	97
Fi Mi God Dey Yah	98
BLESSED WITH ANOTHER DAY	100
CLEAN OUT THE CLOSET	101
CAN YOU HANDLE ME	103
MISSING YOU	106
KEEP YOUR HEAD	107
BE ANGRY AND SIN NOT	108
BREAK UP THE FALLOW GROUND	109
FOLLOW GOD WHOLEHEARTDLY	111
FEED MY SHEEP	113
PRAY AND ASK THE LORD	116
HE WHO BEGAN	117
CREATIVE JUICES	118
ANOTHER WEEK	119
GRACE TODAY	120

AS LONG AS YOUR THERE	121
PLAYERS IN THE PULPIT	123
When You Think	125
May He Make His Face to Shine	126
I WRITE BECAUSE	127
MEN OF GOD ARISE	128
SAINTS BEWARE	131
WHO CAN FATHOM GOD'S WAYS	133
WHERE ARE YOU GOING?	135
GIVE IT TO JESUS	137
HE'S COMING BACK AGAIN	138

Preface

Acknowledgments: To my parents Dad, will love you always. Mother you're my inspiration and strength, thank you. To my brother Errol your humour is good medicine. Clive your support knows no bounds. To other siblings; Bev, Maxcine, Derrick, Keith and family love you all dearly. To Pastor Lennox Greenaway stay humorous and humble .To you my closest friends who know who you are, you are all loved much, and truly appreciated. To Bishop Michael Wilson thank you for pricking me to publish ...your belief in me has been unwavering. To Pastor Errol Williams for empowering others. Pastor Delaney Brown, keep teaching, your labour is not in vain...and stay real. Thank you all.

Aims: My purpose in writing this book was to put together a collection of poems and meditations to inspire, motivate, encourage, and uplift you whoever you are, whatever walk of life you come from, whatever you are going through. Each one has been written from the heart, while facing obstacles such as; grief, illness, and through some of the darkest and challenging moments of my life. Yet through it all, God has been walking with me, and He is walking with you too.

About the author: Born into a family of eight, five boys and three girls, Sharon is the youngest of her siblings. Through having a passion for fashion gaining a Higher National Diploma in Clothing, she has worked in retail management, fashion design and interior design fields. Having always had a love of writing and reading, her other interests include art, cooking, cake decorating, socialising with friends and is known for having a good sense of humour. Previously working as a Youth Mentor Coordinator and Care Croup Pastor in her home church, Church of God of Prophecy- Wembley, and loves continually encouraging people.

"…write the vision, and make it plain upon the tablets that he may run who reads it "Habakkuk 2v1

"You may not see the talent that lies within you, but you should realise others do. Yet it is only when these *few* help you to fulfil your potential, you can move forward and therefore encourage and empower someone else to do the same" – *Sharon. A. Franklin*

"But You O Lord are a God full of compassion, and gracious, longsuffering, and abundant in mercy and truth" Psalm 86 v15

Christ within You

May today the beauty of Christ be seen in you,
That you be a blessing as you bless others around you.
May you have joy where there is much sorrow,
That you find light at the end of the darkness.

May you know the true love of God deep down in your heart,
That you be loved by those around you, as you love others.
May you be healed in your body, mind, soul, and spirit,
That you prosper in all you do.

May you continue to praise the Lord,
That you be obedient to His will.
May you be led by the Holy Spirit,
That you may continue to seek the face of the living God.

May you wait on the Lord and be patient,
That your days will be full of giving Him the praise.
May you smile on through the face of adversity,
That you will show others the God of your salvation.

The Sun will shine again

You've cried, the tears come streaming down,
Upon your face you wear a frown.
You feel you'll never see the sun,
But you should realise the victory is already won.

God he will make you smile again,
Amidst your pain and tears.
You must believe that He is there,
Just cast on Him your cares.

Pains of Life

Lord I don't know,
Which road to go.
Feels like I'm so done in,
Keep wondering if I'll win.
This battle that I'm going through,
Let me now give it all to you.
For this pain in my life,
That I currently feel.
Father this I know; only you can heal.
My mind, my heart, my soul,
I'm longing for you to control.
Lift this heavy burden please,
When Satan tries to tempt and tease.
I know if I but give to you,
My mind, my heart, my soul,
You will renew once more.
For only in your loving arms,
In love and peace I am restored.
These pains of life will pass away,
In you I live, I breathe today,
Amidst the pains of life.

"Beloved do not think it strange concerning the fiery trial which is to try you, as though some strange thing happened to you; but rejoice to the extent that you partake of Christ's sufferings, that when His glory is revealed, you may also be glad with exceeding joy" 1 Peter 4:12-13

MORNING BREAKS

As I open my eyes in the morning,
I'm in awe of a brand new dawning.
Seeing a new day break,
Just as I open my eyes and I'm awake.
Seeing God's wonderful creation,
Unfold before me across all nations.
Sunrise calls in a new day,
Yesterday is come and passed away.
The birds sing in a new dawn,
Sweet harmonies to one and all.
As I breathe in I'm thankful for the day,
A new morning facing challenges along the way.
His glorious creation has such great appeal.
My spirit feels free as the wind in my hair,
When I open my window to the sounds I hear.
Morning breaks, another day I'm thankful for,
On the wings of God's love, today I'll soar.
Thanking God for another day,
As I walk along my way.

BE STILL and know

Be still and know that HE IS GOD,
He is God alone, ruling on His throne.
He sees all, hears all, knows all things,
To Him come lay your burdens down.
Leave them their and go on your way,
Your life He'll straighten out, just pray.
To the Most High God who loves us still,
Just rest, remain, abide in His will.
And be still and know that HE IS GOD.

"I will both lie down in peace, and sleep; For You alone, O LORD, make me dwell in safety" Psalm 4:8

When Sickness Comes

The pain I think will never leave,
As I take a sigh, and I heave.
Can I take it anymore?
Oh Lord I need you to restore.

Renew; revive me now Lord I pray,
Oh that this pain would go away.
How much more can I take?
Sometimes I wish I weren't awake.

To sleep away the pain I feel,
My Lord, dear Lord is this for real?
To each of us, you give what we can bear,
Oh Father God why do I fear?

In sickness I know you are present,
Your awesome power so omnipotent.
When sickness in my life appears,
I will not doubt, God calms my fears.

"Yet I will rejoice in the LORD, I will joy in the God of my salvation. The LORD GOD is my strength; He will make my feet like deer's feet. And He will make me walk on my high hills" Habakkuk 3:18-19

LIVE. LIFE....LAUGH

Live LIFE ....TO THE FULL,
In Him you can laugh until...
He makes you smile so very much,
His love abides with just one touch.

Laughter is....good medicine,
Fantastic for my system.
So live each day, as it's your last,
God laughs with you ...He laughs last.

The Peace of God

Jehovah Shalom, some say He is,
Our peace in this road of life,
We need the peace of God.

A peace that calms the fears of man,
And dwells way down within,
We need the peace of God.

When troubles arise in our lives,
We have an assurance in Him we abide,
We need the peace of God.

"Great peace have those who love your law, And nothing causes them to stumble" Psalm 119:165

OVERWHELMED

Overwhelmed by His presence,
Overwhelmed by His grace,
Overwhelmed by His love,
In every breath that I take,
I am overwhelmed by God.

Overwhelmed by His life,
Overwhelmed by His death,
Knowing that for me He was crucified,
I am overwhelmed by God.

Overwhelmed by His mercy,
Overwhelmed by His peace,
I am overwhelmed by God.

"I remembered God, and was troubled; I complained, and my spirit was overwhelmed" Psalm 77:3

A Mothers' Love

When I was a little child,
Mothers prayers I'd hear at night.
Covering her children in love.
Pleading with Heavenly Father above,
To keep, and to protect her flock.
From the snare of the fowlers shock.
He who seeks to kill and to destroy,
The precious children God has employed…
Her with, to nurture and to love,
Planting precious seeds of life from above.
Training each one of us in the word daily,
That we might know Him plainly.
Mother I can still here you praying,
Sweet conversations with God you were saying.
Thanking Him for your children each day,
That we would walk on the straight way.
Praying that we would one day know,
The Fathers love, He daily shows.
Thank you mother for the love you gave.
Helping us to seek His face.

"Her children arise up and call her blessed…" Proverbs 31:28

To the ruby in my life, the strength that makes me who I am…Mother xxx

"Never say you can't always say you'll try "– Mrs Esmie Franklin

FAMILY MATTERS

God created the family,
Brother, sisters in unity.
Must grow in love and in care,
For one another, as we daily share.
The family it matters, to each and all.
A cord of love that must not be broken,
It is the hearts string of love's token.
To care for each other, no matter,
Through sunshine, rain, or stormy weather.
Through tears, heartache and disagreement,
God's love should be the main ingredient.
To knit us together in unity and love,
That is why God created the family.
We must nurture it so it does not break,
Causing each one terrible heartache.
Family matters yes it does
Remain faithful one to another.
Grounded in love, from above.
Family matters to us all,
So love God and each other,
So it will not fall.

Dedicated to the heartbeats that make up a part of me… love you all for your words of life, love, laughter, and encouragement xxx

PEACE

Peace in the midst of a storm,
He gives peace to a heart torn.
Broken, beaten, and battered to rise no more,
Heavenly Father alone will restore,
Peace while all around is turmoil.
Strife and bitterness all around,
Tears and pain alone to be found,
But God speaks peace to it all.
He gives peace when you've fallen short,
Repent, be restored, He is there.
Your heaviest burden, He can bear.
Peace he will give, so abide in Him,
The battle is His, in victory you will win.

"You will keep him in perfect peace, whose mind is stayed on You." Isaiah 26:3

TRIALS COME TO MAKE YOU STRONGER

Amidst the every day trials you face,
Realise you are not walking alone.
God is forever beside you,
Looking down from His heavenly throne.

Trials come to the best of us,
Regardless of age, gender, or race.
So who do you turn to at these times?
When you fight on and run life's race.

Trials come to make you strong,
Whether you feel weak or have failed at times.
God only gives to each one of us,
What he knows we can handle every time.

LOVE IS PATIENT

Love is not a game of chance,
It is not luck, but it is patient.

Love endures all things it faces,
Prayerfully waits as it unfolds, love is patient.

Love is not to be hurried along,
Like the air of spring, it plays many songs,
Love is …patient.

Love is KIND and TRUE,
In God's time it comes to you,
Wait because ….love is patient.

"Love suffers long and is kind; love does not envy; love does not parade itself, is not puffed up…bears all things, believes all things, hopes all things, endures all things… love never fails" 1 Corinthians 13:4, 7, 8

I HUNGER FOR YOU

It's not food I desire,
Holy Spirit you inspire,
Lord I hunger for you.

In the middle of my day,
Teach me, guide me, I pray,
Lord I hunger for you.

Father do you know, how I love you so,
Help me continually grow,
Lord I hunger for you.

Let me always seek you first,
As I worship, adore and thirst,
Lord I hunger for you.

" *But you, when you pray, go into your room, and when you have shut the door, pray to your Father who is in the secret place, and your father who sees in secret will reward you openly"* Matthew 6:6

DAMSEL ARISE

Damsel arise, arise God says,
You must wake up and tred.
Your feet be ordered by the Lord,
Walking and abiding in His word.

You say you'll never rise again,
As you sleep needlessly in pain.
In Him who paid the ultimate sacrifice,
You can by faith complete this life.

The Father knows the pain you feel,
At times you feel you want to squeal.
Look up to God when things seem bleak,
And place your burden at His feet.

THE LOVE OF GOD

For me He came to this earth,
In order I would be rebirthed.
He paid the price upon the cross,
Loved us so much, He paid the cost.

The love of God runs deep and wide,
Within His arms we can abide.
God loves us all regardless of race,
His love is like amazing grace.

A love that is so pure and true,
He paid the price He died for you.
Within the love of God I'll stay,
To see Him, and remain with him one day.

LIFE GOES ON

When you are in distress,
Call upon Him, you'll be blessed.
Whatever you are going through,
Life goes on ....

Life goes on amidst it all,
Sometimes your up, sometimes you'll fall.
But God will always see you through,
He leads; He cares, and walks with you.

Life goes on, because it must,
If only in God you would completely trust.
In His loving arms you can abide,
For GOD WILL always be your guide.

HE KNOWS IT ALL

In the middle of the night,
Father God hears my cries.
Sees my heart where there is pain,
And restores me once again.
He who formed me in my mother's womb,
Paid the price on the cross,
And with power arose from the tomb.
He knows what is to feel pain,
When nailed to the cross and bloodstained;
Carried my sins and that of the world,
Yes my God knows it all.
I cannot hide one thing from Him,
Even the very simplest of sin;
He sees and He knows all things.
He created heaven and earth,
Every star in the heavens He named,
Our heavenly Father remains the same.
Victorious, triumphant, omnipotent king,
Forever your praises I'll lovingly sing.
You alone see the inward part of me,
In all its flaws and entirety.
You see the dreams, my hearts desires,
Knowing all things are in your Heavenly hands,
You know the plans you have for me;
Though sometimes your ways I cannot see.
I must concede each time I feel,
That I know best, to my knees I fall;
Calling on you to forgive me still,
For in your ways I know I'm blest.

Dear Lord you paid the price for me,
That I would reign with you in eternity,
Yes Lord….you know it all.

"For I know the thoughts that I think toward you, says the LORD, thoughts of peace and not evil, to give you a future and a hope. Then you will call upon me and go and pray to Me and I will listen to you" Jeremiah 29:11-12

It is FINISHED

It is finished He said,
As the crimson blood ran from His side.
As He hung on the cross,
For the sins of the world He was being crucified.
Crying out to the Father;
"Forgive them they know not what they do".
Our Lord Jesus, the Son of God,
Was only willing to die for me and for you.
As He cried out body in pain,
"Father into thy hand I commend my spirit ".
Fearful He was, yet God gave Him the power to do it.
Nevertheless He still questioned and said;
"My God, my God why have you forsaken me?"
The answer God gave, He was to be risen,
For the sake of humanity.

"For God so loved the world that He gave his only begotten Son, that whosoever
believeth in him should not perish, but have everlasting life" John 3:16

Thank you

Father I thank you for today,
For blessing me with victory.
You are my Heavenly King,
My dearest friend,
Lover of my soul.
When I thirst for your spirit,
You quench my thirst.
When I'm down and depressed,
Feel beaten up and worthless.
You send your Heavenly angels,
To encamp about me.
You lighten the heavy burden I carry,
And you make me victorious over my adversaries.
I thank you my Jehovah Jireh,
I love you my precious Lord.
You alone are my strength,
The lamb that was slain for me.
My friend, my healer, my deliverer,
You are my strong tower, thank you.
Even when I am undeserving of your love,
You love me still.
This person who sometimes feels;
Downtrodden, and unworthy in your sight.
Yet you still continue to be the light of my life.
Without you there would be darkness,
A life so empty and useless.
Lord I thank you for loving all of me,
Here I am just as you created me to be.

You alone see my faults and weaknesses,
Your love covers me in all things.
THANK YOU!!

OUTSIDE THESE WALLS

Every Sunday I go to church,
To give God praise and glory.
When outside these walls,
Is it another story?

Do people see in me,
The love of God within?
Who saved me from the pit of hell,
And cleansed my soul from sin.

Outside these safe walls of church,
People are hungry and crying.
Will we feed them with God's love,
Or will we leave them dying?

Slaves to sin they're living in,
Help me dear Lord a soul to win.
Outside these walls I must proceed,
To save a dying soul in need.

"And the gospel must first be preached to all nations" Mark 13:10

Keep LOVING

Keep loving, keep living,
Keep blessing, keep laughing.
Keep crying, don't ever stop praying.
Believing that with God, you can,
Do all things, He's MORE than able

STAND STRONG

His word says in Him abide,
When the storms of life arise.
We can find strength in Him alone,
Who reigns supremely on the throne.

He gives us strength for each new day,
Within His peace, His love…I cannot stray.
When my adversary makes me quite weak,
Upon my knees, His face I'll seek.

We can stand strong when on this race,
If we but always seek God's face.
His strength abides among us still,
We have victory when we abide in His will.

Wait on the LORD

Wait on the Lord, I hear you say,
Patience is the key and the way.
God has the answers you see,
Wait as you pray and you plea.

Wait on the Lord His way is true,
God will always abide with you.
Think not to go on your own way,
Failure will come to you when you stray.

Wait on the Lord He loves you,
Trials build character and help you grow.
God wants the best for me and you,
Wait…wait on the LORD.

"Rest in the LORD, and wait patiently for Him….." Psalm 37:7

Take Time Out for Others

Listen to others, while they talk to you,
Love and you too will be loved in return,
Take time out for others.

Don't just think of yourself only,
Always remember, the sick, lost and lonely,
Take time out for others.

Treat others as you'd like to be treated,
Even when they've lied, cheated and you feel mistreated,
Pray for them…and still take time out for others.

No one told you life would be easy,
Just enjoy the ride live, cry, laugh even when you feel lonely,
Still take time out for others.

Love your family as they are and your friends,
Sometimes life has its ups, downs and some bends,
Still take time out for others.

Never forget your Creator, it is He who made you,
Always give Him the praise for He died for you,
Just take time out for others.

"to godliness brotherly kindness and to brotherly kindness love " 2 Peter 1:7

Smile on

SMILE ...God is with you,
Why do you frown along the way?
Blessed with life to see a new day,
SMILE ...God is with you.

SMILE...though your heart breaks still,
Knowing your safe in His will.
After the tears joy will come,
SMILE ON ... God is with you.

SMILE...GOD IS WITH YOU,
Reigning still on His Heavenly throne.
One day to call Heaven your home.
So SMILE on...GOD IS with YOU.

When GOD GIVES

When GOD gives, it is well given,
When GOD loves you're well loved.
When GOD saves, HE keeps.
When He blesses you NO MAN can curse you.
When HE gives you victories just remember....
NO WEAPON formed against you can prosper,
When man judges you, He is your advocate.
Men must hold there peace, you are his child.
HE KNOWS those who are truly his.

PRAISE HIM

PRAISE HIM… because He woke you up this morning,
Praise Him… for His everlasting mercies.
Praise Him… because weeping may endure for a night,
But you know that joy is coming in the morning.

PRAISE HIM…because He laid down His life for you,
Praise Him… He paid the price for our sins on the cross.
Praise Him… for by His blood we are redeemed,
Praise Him …because He is the author and finisher of our faith.

PRAISE HIM … there is no other God like him,
Praise Him …who paid for our sins on the cross.
Praise Him … he is the great physician,
Praise Him … there is deliverance in praise.

PRAISE HIM … because he is a wonderful counsellor,
Praise Him … he is Jehovah Jireh our provider.
Praise Him … he is El-Shaddai, God Almighty,
Praise Him … he is El-Elyon, the God Most High.

Just praise Him …

Hang on in there

It's not over till God says so,
Hang on in there, keep smiling through.
Cry on, pray on, praise you're not alone.
Hang on in there, you'll come through,
Don't give up the fight.

LORD YOU ARE

LORD YOU, you are,
Holy Father I adore you.
I abide in you,
You are …. The lover of my soul,
Wonderful counsellor to all,
My healer, my guide.
You are …the one, who speaks life to my soul,
Jehovah Jireh my provider,
Jehovah Shalom you alone are my peace.

LORD you are…. my strength when I am weak,
And all around me lays destruction.
You are … my hope,
You alone give me a new song,
When tears are the only language I know.
You are …the light of my life,
My shield, my strong tower.
You are…the Master creator,
In whom we live, we move and have our being.

You are … the sunshine in my smile,
You walk along side me,
When I feel alone.
You are …. The breath of life,
Giving me the courage and power to go on.
LORD you are ….
My deliverer my every heart beat.
Every new song I sing is because of you.

You are …. The wind beneath my feet,
That keeps me in the stillness of the night.
LORD you are …. Awesome, omnipotent, giver of life,
You are …..

As the tears fall

As the tears fall,
Know that He is waiting to dry every one.
God he understands you,
Better than yourself, He holds the master plan.

As the tears fall,
Don't be afraid to come into His presence.
He sees your pain,
Because He is omnipresent.

As the tears fall,
Father God is right there by your side.
He is walking with you always,
Cry on He wants to be your guide.

As the tears fall,
Angels in heaven cry with you.
For the pain you feel is real.
But God will make you smile,
He alone will heal.

BETTER DAYS ARE COMING

What does not kill you,
Only makes you stronger,
It is so often said.
But while you are troubled,
Consider this each time you tred.
Better days are coming,
Open your eyes to see.
Coming over the horizon,
One day you'll have the victory.

Better days are coming,
In the meantime, please don't give up,
When the fight has just begun.
Stand strong within the storm,
The victory will be won.
With patience and in virtue,
It's just a test for you.
Better days are coming,
Our God sticks to His word.
You've prayed, you've cried, you're hurting,
Keep standing, live the word!

Better days are coming,
Just pray, and seek His face.
He'll give you strength,
You have the power,
To overcome and win this race!

" ....let us run with endurance the race that is set before us" Hebrews 12:1

There is a Blessing awaiting YOU

You ask God, why must you go through?
Heart torn apart, feeling so defeated.
Finances broken in two thinking what now,
Dear Lord can't take no more.

Know your blessing is on its way,
But you must persevere and pray.
Though you don't feel like it right now,
How else do you anticipate gaining your crown?

A blessing is awaiting you,
It's just around the corner.
But God requires you to go through,
In order to pursue the blessing awaiting you.

"..and I will cause showers to come down in their season; there shall be showers of blessing" Ezekiel 35:26

The Secret place of God

Where is your hiding place?
In whose arms to abide?
Soaring as on eagles wings you arise,
Abiding in the secret place.

A sanctuary where you retreat,
To meet the Saviour.
Coming into his presence while on your knees,
As Father God he hears your pleas.

He's giving his angels charge over you,
Have you made your dwelling place?
That you might find amazing grace,
Dwelling with him in the secret place.

*"He who dwells in the secret place of the Most High shall abide under the shadow of the Almighty. I
will say of the LORD 'He is my refuge and my fortress; My God in Him I will trust'. Psalm 91:1-2*

Sleep ON

SLEEP on … death is but for a while,
You are asleep in the arms of God,
Patiently resting away from this earth.

Sleep on … be not afraid of the darkness,
Death has no sting …
We remember, your love, and care.

Be at peace and rest awhile,
Sleep on uncle… sleep on,
Away from the pain and strife of this world.

Sleep on … we remember you today,
We pray for your soul that you find rest,
And in heaven…one day we will meet.

Sleep on … as God has called you home,
Though sad we may now be,
One day we will have to take.

This path that you now tread,
Sleep on… uncle sleep on,
In peace into the distant shore of heaven.

"The LORD is near unto them that are of a broken heart…." Psalm 34 v 18

In memory of Uncle Ronald Brown and also my dear cousin Junior, also dear Dad, beloved nephew Adrian and Uncle Fitzy, whose presence is missed but sweet memories linger on and all those no longer with us ... sleep on xx

A FATHERS love

My children know that I am your Father,
Who is always here to guide you,
Love you, on whom you can depend.

To uplift you and encourage you,
In every situation, you go through,
I am your one true friend.

Your Father who stands by you,
Through good times and the bad,
Who loves to hear you laugh, and dries your tears when sad.

My love for you is everlasting,
Since the time before your birth,
You are a special treasure; I've created here on earth.

I see in you great things to come,
Keep shining like the morning sun,
Reach out and know I'm always here.

Your Father that is who I am,
Come… run to me I hold the key,
You have a Father's love in me.

"A father of the fatherless……." Psalm 68:5

To Whom Much is GIVEN

To whom much is given,
Much is expected,
The Lord says so.

What you go through,
It is only a test,
Intended for you to grow.

Growth is a necessity,
Throughout life's complexities,
So go ahead keep trying.

God is with you,
All things are possible in Him,
Just keep on believing.

GODS LOVE

G = grace, gentle, gracious
O = omniscient, overcome, overjoyed
D = devotion, dynamic, divine
S = satisfying, salvation, strong

L = life changing, lyrical, loyal
O = outstanding, omnipotent, overflows
V = versatile, valuable, victorious
E = exceptional, everlasting, ecstatic

Your LOVE

Your love abides with me,
Your hope fills me
Your peace keeps me
Your light leads me

HIS GRACE & PEACE

Nothing can be sweeter,
Than amazing grace,
God gives to us.
His grace saves us,
It just keeps washing over us,
Nothing can be greater.
Than sweet peace in our souls,
It calms our fears,
Our minds, our hearts.
Only His grace and peace,
Can saturate us still,
While daily living, always giving,
And abiding in His will.
Only his grace and peace,
Can touch the inward part of man,
Enabling Him to understand.
His grace reveals,
His peace it heals,
A tortured soul within.

"My grace is sufficient for you, for My strength is made perfect in weakness"
2 Corinthians 12:9

"For He himself is our peace......" Ephesians 2:14

The Battle is His

The battle is His
The victories are won
In Him we learn to overcome

What is FAILURE?

F = falling down and getting back up again

A = ascending and soaring to greater heights

I = inspired to do better

L = loved by God regardless

U = undaunted by shortcomings

R = resurrected from defeat

E = empowered to succeed

"But I have prayed for you, that your faith should not fail ….." Luke 22:32

Till Thy Kingdom Come

Souls to win for your kingdom,
Thy will always to be done.
Prayerfully waiting, anticipating on you,
Till dear Lord thy kingdom comes.

He Who Died for You

How many people do you know?
That would die for you?
Would feel the pain and the agony,
Facing the tragedy upon the cross,
To save your soul from being lost.
The price was paid for me and you,
A pain that only He went through.
We cannot ever comprehend,
So deep a love from any friend?
Who would die for you on Calvary?
So that you might live in eternity,
Once away from the pains and strife,
Here on earth, in this life.
Jesus paid the price for you,
That one day you would see,
Just what your purpose, was meant to be.
Living and giving Him the praise,
Continually being lifted, in His love raised.
How many people do you know?
Who love you and would die for you?

"and He died for all, that those who live should live no longer for themselves, but for Him who died for them and rose again" 2 Corinthians 5 v 15

Holy Spirit Seal Me

Holy Spirit I need to be sealed in you,
Your words to inspire,
Your spirit to lean onto.
Holy Spirit you speak,
You lead and you guide.
Ever present with me,
Daily you uphold me.
Teach me the ways of the Lord,
To be sealed in your ways,
Ever shining bright in you.
My heart to be clean,
Take not your Holy Spirit from me.
God knows I need you,
I need your sweet fragrance,
To daily carry me through.

"In Him you also trusted, after you heard the word of truth, the gospel of your salvation; in whom also, having believed you were sealed with the Holy Spirit of promise" Ephesians 1:13

FRIENDSHIP

True friendship is a gift from above,
Wrapped deeply in the Father's love.
The art of sharing with another,
God's love manifesting in sisters and brothers.

The love of a good friend is always felt,
In times of trials and adversities.
The grace of God still carries on,
Amidst life's daily travels.

Sometimes friends may disagree,
It's just a test of life.
True colours will then surface,
During this brief moment of time.

Thoughts shared, encouragement given,
The spirit enables you to discern.
What did I say, what did I do?
To make them behave the way they do.

Some friends come into your life,
Having their purpose to play.
Some will masquerade as a friend,
Only to curse you and fall away.

To these take heed and be warned,
Father God knows and sees the heart.
Pray for them, fear not at all,
The Lord will enable you to stand tall.

Others leave footprints to be inspired,
A word of life spoken, when tired.
Can uplift the weary soul of man,
When you feel others care and understand.

Understanding your need for a shoulder,
To cry on, pray with and bolster you.
The true characteristics of a friend,
Should then be visible to view.

Loyalty, trust, care and honesty,
Loving through adversity, life's complexities.
Forgiveness when having been wronged,
Knowing when to hold your tongue.

Speaking life not death to the situation,
Aspiring you to rise far above your expectations.
Enfolding you in thoughts and prayer,
Not wanting you to fail in your endeavours.

Integrity, a praying spirit, kindness,
Wisdom to know when to be silent.
Grace, laughter and smile warming the heart,
Transparency ensues for all to see.

Thoughts shared, confidences kept,
Lives walking in the Fathers footsteps.
Truth displayed without contest,
Competing against each other....no.

But, as the word says love at all times,
One whose their with you through storms,
Disappointments, grief, discouragement, failure,
Without a bitter word or snipe.

The love of God being evident,
His presence always omnipotent.
Friendship is a gift from God above,
So establish good friendships in the Lord.

People whom you can rely on,
To pray, esteem, encourage and motivate.
When words of life dictate,
Touching the inner core of you.

"I have called you friend..." John 15:15

Dedicated to the real friends in my life, who know who you are and how valued you are ... thank you for sharing part of you ... with me :0)

HEAR MY CRY

God of all of me,
Can you hear me?
Do you see the hurt within?
That can't be seen by man.
Lord are you their?
As I'm carrying the cares,
Of the world that are crunching;
Yet on your living word I'm still standing.
Can you hear my cries at night,
As my eyes well up at times.
With my burdens bearing down,
Let me bring them to your feet.
Leaving it there as I look up,
Heavenly Father …hear my cry,
Fill my cup ….

ON ANGEL WINGS

On angel wings I'm lifted,
Soaring high, high up,
Meeting God in the morning.
Angelic magnificence displayed,
In the presence of God, I'm amazed.

ALL I NEED

Jesus is all I need,
My hungry soul to feed.
In Him I'll always be abiding,
His grace and love just keeps me smiling.

ONLY YOU

Only you see my heart when others do not,
Or cannot see the inward part of me.
The heart, in which from you cannot be hidden,
My deepest thoughts are uncovered.
You see what you want me to be,
Amidst what I think is uncertainty.
To love, when love is not given,
Yet your word drives me to care.
Walking where angels fear to tread,
Giving a word to a hungry soul.
Though I want to go in a different direction,
Your love Lord pulls me in wisdom.
To walk and talk the narrow way.
My righteous Lord how can I stray.
Move away from what you want of me,
Thy glory Lord for all to see.
When it comes down to it anyway;
It's only what we do for you, or say,
Will last the test of time in testament.
The works of the spirit evident,
Praising you dear Lord in your brightness.
Our hearts be lifted up showing kindness,
Love, compassion to those who know you not.
Our life should be a witness to the lost,
Only you see the very make up of man,
Where lies abound, when truth should stand.
Yet your grace covers a multitude,
To saint or sinner of any race,
Lord Jesus let us love, seeking your face.

"I am the first and I am the last; and beside me there is no God "Isaiah 44:6 KJV

When God Is Silent

When God is silent, what does it mean?
That in His omnipotence, He has not heard,
He does not see your pain, your need.

It does not mean he does not care,
About your situations in this life,
He's God of course He sees.

Yet in this busy, busy world,
Sometimes the Father needs,
For us to wait upon Him earnestly.

Not hurrying to our own tune,
But awaiting the essence of,
The still small voice of His.

Silence, with patience is great,
Disciplining you as you wait,
Taking God at His word.

So that we do not act independently,
Outside of His will, the life He,
Has given to walk in oneness with Him.

For God is always patient, and kind,
Always having our best interest in mind,
Knowing the end result is His perfection.

So wait on the Lord having asked,
His will for your life will last,
The test of time, His love endures.

NEVER GIVE UP

You can't see the light right now,
All around darkness it permeates.
Wondering if you'll see daybreak,
Needing the Holy Spirit to saturate.
Feeling like you'll never succeed,
But never give up, with Jesus you'll be,
Soon singing sweet songs of victory!
Never give up, even when in the midst,
Though it feels like you can't catch,
The very air you try to breathe;
It's as though it's contaminated by the adversaries schemes.
God won't leave you in your distress,
He's waiting right now to sort out your mess.
The sweet blessing the Lord will bestow,
When the breakings over, sweet blessings will flow.

"Yea, the Lord shall give that which is good; and our land shall yield her increase. Righteousness shall go before him; and shall set us in the way of his steps" Psalm 85:12-13 KJV

IT'S NOT ABOUT ME

It's not about me,
It's your glory they need to see.
Blazin forth from within,
Shining your light onto men.

FORGIVENESS

F = fathered by Him
O = omnipotent Father
R = reality bites
G = grateful for His mercies
I = inspired by the word
V = vindicated by truth
E = encouraged in His grace
N = notable in His presence
E = eternal God is our refuge
S = sanctified perspective
S = salvation is free to all

WHO AM I?

I am heir to a Heavenly kingdom,
Combined of princes and princesses of godly wisdom.
Walking in power and substance,
Under my kings covering and guidance.

My king is the owner of the earth moon and stars,
Created by Him, as He breathed life by His word.
How can I but walk less than who I am,
An heir of righteousness within Christendom.

Like a rough diamond hewed,
He bought me, by His precious blood.
Yet I still have kinship with Him,
Washed and cleansed within the flood.

I am royalty, being born again,
So why should I live less than I am.
In a world of sin and dark despair,
My king controls the very atmosphere.

In which I walk and breathe each day,
For I know I'm fearfully and wonderfully made.
Abounding in my kings grace and glory,
For He alone knows my life story.

From conception in my mother's womb,
My king knows my every thought and move.
His royal eyes search the very heart of me,
Lovingly overseeing my destiny.

I am His, His regal chid,
A living breathing heir to be inspired.
In Him the breath of life in whom I live,
His eminence Most High I daily give.

Praises to my King in all I do,
His holiness abiding and alive in me.
I am the apple of His eye,
I know who I am … Who are you?

"But ye are a royal priesthood, a holy nation …." 1 Peter 2:9 KJV

WALK AWAY

If God is in it stay,
If not you'd better …walk away.
Retreat to go and seek Him first,
He should be your daily thirst.

If He says no, do not proceed,
Or He will bring you to your knees.
It's good to wait upon the Lord,
The blessings He will then outpour.

Things you never thought could be,
Suddenly become a reality.
When He says stop, don't go no further,
Are you so foolish to ignore?

You're sweet King Jesus, who loves you,
To whom all praise, and honour is due.
The Saviour knows what is best for you,
He loves, He cares, and He died for you.

GODS PEACE

G = gentle, good-natured, good-sense
O = obliterates, observant, obtainable
D = dance, delightful, desires
S = satisfies, solemn, sympathises

P = prayerful, precious, promises
E = eternal, everlasting, encourages
A = amazing
C = contentment, calming
E = endures, effective

"He himself is our peace ...." Ephesians 2:14 KJV

FAILURE IS NOT THE END

When you fail it is just another beginning,
To fail is not a disgrace.
You've tried, now get up again,
That's just the adversaries plan.

God has greater things in store,
Look ahead and not back.
He's teaching discipline and grace,
Get up, move on, and don't stay down on your face.

Think positive you will get through,
God is just pruning you.
For what He has in store,
You need the character to accept it.

He's leading you to deeper heights,
Don't you dare forget it.
When the breakthrough arises,
Shout praises and accept it !

The storm that you went through,
Was just a test built just for you.
When He is finished moulding you,
You'll shine; you'll smile on …..

SORRY IS HARD TO SAY

Though we yet live in this world,
Our lives should emanate the word.
Words of love and forgiveness,
For healing pain and sickness.

God sees the very heart of man,
He alone has the master plan.
The words that come out of our mouth each day,
Should be of love in every way.

Though sometimes we may get,
Caught out by the adamic nature.
We then should seek the Master Creator,
So go apologise to those you've hurt.
Humbling yourself will establish …your true worth!

".... I dwell in the high and holy place, with him also that is of a contrite and humble spirit, to revive the spirit of the humble, and to revive the heart of the contrite ones " Isaiah 57:15 KJV

GOD HOLDS ME

God saves me,
He keeps me.
His love enfolds, holding me.
Never ever letting go,
As His Holy Spirit flows.

SO MISUNDERSTOOD

When you don't even know the real reason,
Why not keep your mouth still.
Instead of running them down hill,
All because they said …'no!'

A heart that truly loves the Lord,
Should surely try to be on one accord.
With there fellow man in love and in deed.
You may misunderstand the 'no!'

Not in the context it was intended.
So chide your tongue,
As your friend you'll falsely have misapprehended,
Judge not and you will be judged.

In all you say and do.
So it is we misunderstand…
We skin up, vex up, and get annoyed,
Not asking the real reason for the answer.

Then comes the broken ties of,
Love, and friendship,
While the adversary sits about laughing ….

Think about it!

"The lips of truth shall be established for ever; but a lying tongue is but for a moment" Proverbs 12:19 KJV

HE SAVES HE KEEPS

Divine God you save,
In the middle of failures you keep.
Your loving arms always outstretched,
Comforting me when I'm stretched.

Up, down, around and very which way,
Your grace it covers each day.
Though at times I'm thinking I'm unable,
Your loving arms are always stable.

"O LORD of hosts, blessed is the man that trusteth in thee" Psalm 84:12 KJV

STAY IN HIS PRESENCE

In His presence is fullness of joy,
Abundant peace to be given.
In His presence there is sweet peace,
Joy unspeakable, grace, hope so unbelievable.
His power dominates as,
Fragrance like lilies in the valley,
Emanate so beautifully.
He cares, He loves,
So dearly all His children.
Black, white, all colours of the rainbow,
Each beautifully made by His hands.
Created in His perfect image,
So stay within God's presence,
Where abiding in Him,
Gives strength to the weak.
Hope to the hopeless,
Love to the unloved one.
Faith to the faithless,
He'll provide your deepest need,
Weary souls He'll gladly feed,
Firing you up in the spirit.
While standing on His living word,
So pure and so true.
Living water flowing from His mercy seat,
Jehovah saves, He cares and He keeps.
Amidst the potholes of lives journey,
Father God already knows your life story.
From the beginning of creation,
Plans were made for your elevation.

In the fullness of His time,
Humble yourself, and then He'll exalt you to shine.
Just stay in His presence,
Practise patience and grace,
Through prayer, always seeking His face.
Who promised you everyday would be sunshine!
But nevertheless, God always makes you smile.
From the inward part of man,
Which He alone sees and understands.
The heart from which He dwells deep within,
Wanting us to be completely free from sin.
Yet as the loving father He is,
Gently leads and directs our steps in Him.
Successes turned to failures,
Fear and doubt tries to creep right in,
Yet God comforts you in His arms.
Reassuring you, so you can win!
Trials of life only make you stronger,
So endure go through, and conquer in His name.
Stay in the presence of the Lord,
Remain with Him on one accord.

"You will show me the path of life; in Your presence is fullness of joy; at Your right hand pleasures evermore" Psalm 16:11

BLAZE ON

Holy Spirit blaze in me,
Blinding bright my enemies.
The fire of God emanating from me,
Giving me the victory,
Deliverance songs I'm singing,
As I blaze on in Jesus.

"If He says He will, trust Him. God does not and cannot lie "– Sharon Franklin

SEEK GOD FIRST

Waking in the morning,
I'm giving Him the praise.
Praying to my Heavenly Father,
Thankful for another day.
The very reason I'm created.
His omniscience appreciated.
Praising Him while on my knees,
My God hears my earnest pleas.
I'm seeking Him first in all I do,
With my heart offered up willingly.
Persistently pursuing my King.
Even while walking in adversity.
My King created me divinely,
Breathing His Holy Spirit which inspires.
Gives me power to pursue,
My hungry soul seeking you,
As I continually hunger and I thirst,
I'll always seek my God first.

"There is no fear in love, but perfect love casts out fear...." 1 John 4:18 KJV

Come Lord Jesus...Come

Hungrily I see to see your face,
Transcending glory radiates your grace.
The very thought of seeing you Lord,
My heart to be on one accord.

Jesus you are my soul's desire,
Though the adversary tries to destroy.
The very gifts you've given and employed,
To do your will until you crack the sky.

Divine one in all your radiant glory,
My life in you must be a living story.
Reaching the very heart of sinful man,
In order that I fulfil your master plan.

Come Lord Jesus come to me,
Your Holy Spirit continually captivating.
While praise and worship from me escalates,
Into a thanksgiving dance translating.

The thoughts of what you've done for me,
Words cannot express the harmony.
While when giving you the very best of me,
As I praise you in my sanctuary.

Bended knees or standing I'm shouting,
Of the victories and blessings I'm abounding.
Your Holy Spirit comforts me,
When faced with doubt by the adversary.

Into your arms I come lay down,
When the weight of this world makes me frown.
Your power gives me the ignition needed,
Lighting the fire within and blinding my enemies!

Setting ablaze the love I have for you,
Transcending grace gives me peace.
While those around me want to steal,
My joy, my strength, to you I yield.

Come Lord Jesus come fill me up,
Allowing my cup to run over.
With your anointing just like fire,
Silencing those who think I'm done.

In you dear Lord I overcome,
Every obstacle I daily face.
Upon your word I'm standing still,
Your love and strength encompass me.

Yet Lord when you will return,
Let me be earnestly upon you waiting.
As you find me doing what you called me to,
Telling the world of the goodness of you.

Come Lord Jesus ....Come

"With Him are wisdom and strength, He has counsel and understanding"
Job 12:13 KJV

Love Is a Curious Thing

Pretenders come in all guises,
Spouting flattering words to draw you in.
Is the love of God displayed?
Or is it all game playing?

To love is not to do wrong,
It has melodious overtones.
Of a fragrance sweet and fair,
When embarking, do take care!

Love is a curious thing,
Make sure God is always in.
Every moment, step you take,
Don't let satan dominate.

What you do, how you act,
As heirs of the king should not distract,
You from walking in integrity,
Respecting each other in decency.

Treating her like the lady she is,
Esteeming him as a man of God.
Keeping God at the centre of all choices,
He'll then bless you with great reward.

Don't let the adversary cause you to sin,
When fallen down its hard to get up again.
So walk in wisdom, love and grace,
Letting the Saviour set your pace.

"I therefore the prisoner of the Lord, beseech you to walk worthy of the calling with which you were called" Ephesians 4:1 KJV

Tears

T = trials always make you stronger
E = everlasting God reigns supreme
A = abiding in His presence
R = restored in God's arms
S = strength after wiping weeping eyes

"It's in the valley we grow, so praise on in the valley, and you'll soon see the mountain top "– Sharon. A .Franklin

Peace

P= passes all human understanding
E= eternal love of God
A= abundant joy in Him be found
C= Christ the hope of the world
E = enlightened in the knowledge of Him

Hope

H= happy in God
O= omnipresent Lord
P = passion for Christ
E = eternal life with Him

I'm Tired

I'm tired....yet you say STAND,
I'm tired yet Lord you love me still.
Telling me that I can overcome,
As I endure and go on in your will.

I'm tired ....can't see the daylight,
Monies tight, creditors haunting my nights.
I'm tired....yet you say PRAY ON,
As I rise up stronger to fight.

I'm tired....sickness does not want to leave,
Father God hold me, to you I cleave.
You are my divine healer,
In your living word I'm relieved.

I'm tired....success turned to failure,
Feeling downtrodden but not out for the count.
As I cry unto thee with a loud plea,
You comfort me secure in your arms.

I'm tired ....thinking when will I see the light,
Life looks dark, as the darkest midnight.
Yet I hear your still small voice Lord,
Telling me to go on, press on.

That I can rise up on eagles wings,
Singing sweet songs of jubilation.
Having gone through trials, tribulations,
Your footsteps guide in you I'm hiding.

Safe in the Masters care at all times,
The adversary trying to conquer.
But your Holy Spirit makes me stronger,
Enabling me to rise up triumphantly!

"He gives power to the weak and to those who have no might He increases strength" Isaiah 40:29

Enlarge my Territory

Upon you and your word I'm standing,
Seeking after the heart of you.
Your love sustains as little becomes much,
When placed in your hands dear Lord.

Looking to you the father of life an light,
Shining and burning bright in the heart of me.
Blazin and firing me up in you,
As you order my footsteps and take my hand.

Enlarging my coast for your kingdom,
That should be my first priority.
Seeking to give you praise and glory,
Your living words my sustenance.

Abiding in you, blessings abundance,
Will follow my path on this journey.
Lord of hope and giver of life,
Be thine my continual victor.

".....Oh that thou would bless me and enlarge my territory "1 Chronicles 4:10 KJV

MORE LIKE JESUS

More like Jesus,
I want to be.
To have the spirit of,
His grace and humility.

More like Jesus,
I need to see,
Loving all without partiality,
But to be in harmony with all.

More like Jesus,
Girding the fiery tongue.
That kills the inner man,
When harsh words are spoken.

More like Jesus,
To heal the sick and lame.
Not for any fortune,
But to glorify His name.

More like Jesus,
Loving with a pure heart.
The one's whose lives,
Are so torn apart.

Fi Mi God Dey Yah

Fi mi God im real!
Only He could a died pun da cross,
Paying da price an da cost for da lost.

Fi mi God dey yah!
Never fi left me ever,
Greater dan great He is.

No smaddy but Him is so real,
Jesus Christ 'is' da real deal!
A fi we God dat.

Fi mi God won't tek no chupidness,
Come to Him with ya unrighteousness,
He alone will cause you to fix up!

My God im a go give you da victory!
Hold on still sing songs of jubilee,
That's fi wi King Jesus!

No badda tink you can ramp wid Him,
Carry on and play wid fire,
Look see if you nuh get ….bun!

Come to Him…Him a wait pun u and luv u still,
Yes barse …ere wha mi a sey nuh !
Fi wi God dey yah !!!

A patois praise. ..A little jam down flavour :0)

BLESSED WITH ANOTHER DAY

Another day of life oh Lord,
How precious thou hast given me.
I bless Your Name on earth;
The wondrous beauty that I see.
For you are life and light enfolded in the brightness of the sun,
For Lord You are King of Kings the Lamb upon the throne.
O father thou art everything to me ,
My soul rejoices in the blessings you constantly give me.
The air I breathe, eyes to see the earth thou hast created.
That I might live and walk like you; and one day be rewarded.
For YOU ARE life to me,
None other could there ever be,
And I will bless your name for yet another day!

CLEAN OUT THE CLOSET

Into the inward heart of man,
God sees and knows all things.
Creator of the universe,
Nothing can be hidden from Him!

Beyond the outward masquerade,
He see within the soul.
Knowing if we are truly His,
Abiding in Him with our all.

Our minds to be renewed,
Daily living by the word.
The heart must first be cleansed,
Of bitterness and envy at work.

The closet to be sanctified,
Washed over by His spirit.
In order for Him to be,
Vacant and we bear fruit we're His.

Not a fleck not a spot ,
Of worldly ways should be there.
Daily dying each day praying,
Asking God to heal the hurt.

If the vessel of God is full,
Of corruption caused by flesh;
Pride and unconfessed sin to God,

How do we expect to be blessed?

So to each one of us must be,
A change of heart and adoration.
Firstly honoring Father God,
In a true and living fashion!

CAN YOU HANDLE ME

You say you're the one,
Can you handle me?
I am strong righteous woman of God,
Whose first love is for the Lord.

Who's independent of her own mind,
Educated, saturated by God's word.
Articulate, beautiful in this world,
Can you handle me?

Are you strong enough to be my protector?
Shield me, empower me daily.
Or will you rant unnecessary,
As I progress professionally.

Can you handle the fact?
I'm not going to be your doormat.
To be stepped on as required,
Not to speak or be inspired.

That as a strong woman of integrity,
I'll only submit to you equally.
As we both humble ourselves in His presence,
Obeying the word, as God is omnipotent.

Seeing the very heart of man,
As the adversary makes His plans.
I need a prayer warrior beside me,
As we both go forward taking territories.

Abiding in the shadow of God,
Which reaches far and beyond.
There are no limits to HIS ways,
God's love outweighs all earthly gains.
Can you be my strong arms today?
To lift me up when skies are grey.
When days are dark and dreary
Will you be weak and weary?

I know I'm fearfully and wonderfully made,
In the image of my Father created.
Are you solid as the rock of Christ,
Or are you easily shaken and frightened?

When storms of life come raging by,
Do you really qualify?
To be my strong tower, to lift me up,
Or be the one who falls apart.

What I need is a strong man,
Not sum demented weakling.
Who insecure, questions everything,
I say, I do, will that be you?

Or can you handle me?
That I am indelible woman,
Fashioned from the rib of man,
Having the power to stand.

That I will be your righteous queen,

Who upholds, supports you in all things.
The essence of the Creator within me,
Making you see the greatness in you!

Can you handle me?
That as we soar to greater heights,
We grow, in peace, in love and grace,
Forever seeking the Fathers face.

Can you handle me?

MISSING YOU

Where has the time flown?
It seems like yesterday, now gone.
It pleased the Lord to take you home,
Out of sickness and pain onto Heavenly shores.

So loved and missed so much by all,
Your love and laughter stood tall.
Even in the very midst of your pain,
You made us laugh, over and over again.

Though the illness ate away at your flesh,
Your personality and character still manifested.
Stronger some days, weaker on others,
As family and loved ones always hovered.

So out of the pain you're now asleep,
Safe in God's arms your soul to keep.
Sleep well in peace, and out of pain,
Praying we'll meet, one day on that heavenly plain.

"......Blessed are you who weep now, for you shall laugh" Luke 6v 21

KEEP YOUR HEAD

Keep your head in these mad times,
The Lord will still inspire you.
His loving arms will strengthen,
As to Him you come lay your burdens down.

Keep your head in the days ahead,
Hold your tongue, think before you speak.
For what is in the heart,
Is sure to spring forth, sooner or later.

Keep your head in sickness,
God HE knows the pain you're feeling.
He CAN give you healing,
As His loving arms enfold.

Keep your head in financial trials,
Spoils of life are broken down.
Tired, disappointed frown upon your face,
Rest in God's amazing grace!

BE ANGRY AND SIN NOT

Sometimes it's rather difficult,
When faced with all the obstacles.
Once your mouth is open and in full swing,
Is it often speaking Godly things?

Conversations of your fellow man,
Are you praising or cursing them?
These lips can often cause a war,
When words abound over again.

That cannot be taken back,
What's in the heart will surface.
The masquerade revealed at last,
With the tongue you blast your family...

Friends or those who caused you pain,
When all you should do is... pray for them.
Being angry is a natural state,
Try not to let sin translate.

Once vile words have gone forth,
Those you've hurt will feel torn.
That you could be so disheartening,
When sweet words should really be spoken.

To restore the unity that once was,
Rooted and grounded in God's love.
Now lies tattered and broken,
Out of your lips harsh words have been spoken

BREAK UP THE FALLOW GROUND

Tired of being used, abused,
Only when people need or want,
They call, and suddenly your suppose,
To drop everything and come running.

Listening to their wants, their needs,
But can't they see that you're hurt, you need!
That reassurance, a hug, a word to be told, its ok,
It will pass, things will get better…no it's all about self.

It's all about them, what 'they want, how they feel',
You ask yourself the question, 'where is God in this deal?'
Doesn't His word say ***self must decrease* as He increases?**
To love as He loved the church, let's face it He loved so much He died for us!

So how can you continually use and abuse your brothers, sister or brethren?
In such a way it causes them hurt and upset.
You gossip, you slander, and you talk up one another,
Yet with the same mouth you shout amen and hallelujah!

So let me ask you the question; can God be pleased with this?
Can He be honoured by how we dishonour one another?
Where is the love that was slain upon the cross?
The hunger for the lost, rather than prosperity messages.

Everyone into property, and prosperity, whatever happened to prophesy?

Until He comes ....we should preach the gospel to the sad and lost.
Yet souls lay dormant, asleep and some are dying,
As Christians cuss on, pray on, fighting, some are crying.

Over everything else.... except the Saviour who died!
They say they need love in their lives.
Anyhow, anywhere they'll run to get it.
In church, outta church ...desperate to grab it.

While tears from Heaven's mansion doors,
Stroll down to earth from distant shores.
As the one who should be the *one true* lover of man's soul,
Jesus weeps for those who once loved Him so.

As He looks down and sees the inbred fighting,
As demons sit in glee celebrating with themselves.
Yet another church we've contaminated,
Yes, we've come and desecrated.

The Holy tabernacle of the Lord,
We laugh as we now see discord.
The way they're upsetting their one another,
This isn't a church it's now the devils corner.

FOLLOW GOD WHOLEHEARTDLY

Following God takes commitment,
Obeying His true will and ways.
Grace and holiness should be,
Ever glowing from your face.

Stop playing church and awake!
Now is the appointed time.
For every race on earth to arise and shine,
For Christ is coming soon!!

Our lives should be living letters,
Declaring King Jesus our Lord.
Don't compromise, don't tell lies....but
Use the word as a double edged sword.

For the Father knows His children,
Who truly mean business for Him.
So be totally souled out today,
For tomorrow you may never see!!

Follow God with your whole heart,
You only get one chance of life.
They'll be no negotiating on judgement day,
So let the Holy Spirit guide your way.

So work out your own salvation,
Seeking and always thirsting after Him.
Are worldly entices drawing you away?
Return and be restored today!!

For who promised you tomorrow?
If the angel of death was to appear.
Can we each say Lord I'm ready;
I've run my race and persevered?

God sees the inner part of man,
Knows the very content of the heart.
He can revive, renew, restore,
If we are honest from the start!

Let righteousness and holiness arise,
Remove the veil of worldliness from our eyes.
As we the people of the God,
Humbly bow down our will, to yours!!

Come walk with Christ today,
For I say time is short !!
The trumpet of the Lord shall sound,
Then time will be..no more .
Walk worthy with God,
In Spirit and in truth.
Like Enoch did, and David;
Men after God's own heart.

Walk in the light of God

FEED MY SHEEP

Feed my sheep the Lord cries,
To the shepherds that feed themselves.
I the Lord will judge you,
For you've gone against my word.

Feed my sheep the Lord cries,
I desire my people to be fed.
Clothed, and ministered to always,
Just as my word declares.

Feed my sheep the Lord cries,
Don't you know the weak need strength?
They need healing,
Yet you feed yourselves instead!

Feed my sheep the Lord cries,
They have now scattered.
For the rich pasture they once fed on,
Now no longer searches for them.

Feed my sheep the Lord cries,
I desire my people to be fed.
You constantly disobey me,
So you will feel my wrath instead.

I the Lord will repay you,
My heart is torn apart.
You the leaders my shepherds,
Shall feel my judgement on your head.

Yet you have hardened your hearts,
While my sheep have fallen away.
The love of many waxing cold,
As heinous spirits now unfold.

You're feeding yourselves,
Instead of the flock.
Getting fat off the land,
While my sheep die or drop …..

Off to another tabernacle they run,
To get compassion under a new sun.
The fire that once burned bright,
In the shepherds have now turned dim.

Investments, property instead of prophecy,
Finds you wrapped up in confusion.
Who is reaping my harvest?
To include sinners as I planned?

Each have turned their eyes,
My heart cries, I despise;
What you have now become,
Ruling with no vision, this is not my doing!

A den of thieves, like Pharisees,
My tabernacle has now turned into.
For your very own devices,
You've turned to your own vices.

Come back to me, be revived and restored,
Come back to me, your first love.
I will renew you to your former glory,
I paid the price, I AM THE LORD!

Feed my sheep you shepherds,
As they cry out to me.
Go and find the lost,
Who hurt emotionally and spiritually!

They need a word of encouragement,
Not to be further disheartened.
Show love, peace, and compassion;
I the LORD cries. …FEED MY SHEEP!

"Woe to the shepherds that feed themselves! should not the shepherds feed the flocks?" Ezekiel 34 v 2 KJV

"Do you love me" and he said to Him 'Lord you know all things; you know That I love you Jesus said to Him "Feed my sheep" John 21 v 17 KJV

PRAY AND ASK THE LORD

Pray and ask the LORD to deal,
A heart to turn or pain to heal.
He sees, He knows , He understands,
King Jesus has the master plan!

Today is the beginning of a brand new day,
Yesterday has gone, you can't turn back time.
So look ahead to Him, trust GOD as you abide;
Safe in HIS arms He'll make you smile :O)

HE WHO BEGAN

He who began a good work in me, you all a we....
Nuh mus can keep we!
Be blessed not stressed, head up not down;
You'll wear your heavenly crown.

If GOD'S brought you to it, He'll lead you through it,
After the storms comes the showers of blessings.
So stand strong in the knowledge,
There is a King in You!

CREATIVE JUICES

Creative juices flowing in the knowledge of Christ,
I'm glowing Holy Spirit emanating.
As the Fathers love keeps blazing,
So no matter what the adversaries plan;
On Christ the solid rock, You, I, We ...can
Stand ....enjoy this glorious day that GOD has made!

ANOTHER WEEK

Another week to live….to love….to laugh,
To praise, winter, rain or stormy weather,
You are HIS eternal treasure.
Smile :O) GOD's not finished with you yet,
Keep running your race in the midst!

GRACE TODAY

Thanking GOD for grace today,
That kept my peace and paved my way.
As HIS words resound in my spirit,
Peace be still….you can handle it!

AS LONG AS YOU'RE THERE

Feeling your amazing grace,
Holy Spirit emanating all around.
Just to behold your awesome face,
Your royal presence filling the atmosphere.

Cherubim's and Seraphim's bow down in awe,
At the glorious sight of you.
As long as your there,
I'm just thinking about the view.

Crying out to my deliverer, my healer,
Holy One …Hallelujah how wonderful you are!
Seated in Your royal throne,
Power and authority abounding.

As tears fall from my face,
Beholding the wonderful sight of you!
Heaven will be alright,
Jesus as long as you're there!

Just to sit at your feet,
And look at your face.
Feeling your awesome embrace,
Just to be where you are LORD.

Hearing the angels voices in unison,
Singing sweet sounds of jubilation.
Just because you are there,
Glorious sounds of exaltation.

Your amazing peace abounding,
Pain and hurt to cease.
Heaven will be just right...
As long as you're there!!

'Behold the Lamb of God "- John 1:29
Inspired by Donnie McClurkins 'As long As your There'

PLAYERS IN THE PULPIT

Out of the world God's taken you,
Yet you say, you'll do what you wanna do!
Acting up like your all that,
When your attitude should be.

Gratitude…..to God …but you playing,
Sis Mary on Monday, Wendy Tuesday;
Sis Sarah on Wednesday, Sis Barbara Thursday,
Then back in church on Sunday.

Shouting holy roly praises to the Most High,
While heaven cries as tears roll by!
Sisters hurt, used and abused,
As brother player feels ….bemused.

But wait! He's forgotten what the word says,
Old men teach the young to control themselves.
Yet none of this he's awake to,
Only the spirit of self to consume.

Where are the men of standard?
To correct this behaviour.
Not realizing this conduct so…
So grieves the Saviour!

Saying gonna do what He's gonna do,
Don't anybody try stop him.
While some look on, asking..
The Holy Spirit to drop him….

Two lick of repentance fire,
To recondition his heart and mind.
Back out of worldly lust and,
Saturated by the living word.

To show the error of his ways,
At last exposed and no longer hidden.
The grace of God to restore,
Sin confessed to him once more.

Renewing his mind in the living word,
Striving with intent to present,
His body as a living sacrifice;
Restored, rejuvenated, revived... back in Christ!

Players in the house ...fix up!

'Present your body a living sacrifice' – Romans 12v1

When You Think

When you think that nothing is happening,
Think again that's when God is up to something.
Stay in tune with the LORD;
In order to be on one accord,
It's only what you do for Him will last,
Just look to him the victory you'll win.
Trust HIM to do what HE already knows....is best for you!

May He Make His Face to Shine

May God Bless you, may He make,
His face to shine on you always.
May He enlarge your territory!
And establish every good thing;
In you for His purpose.

Order your footsteps in His word,
He'll set your feet on high places.
May your hands prosper and success,
Be in everything you do at all times.

Let God fight the battles,
Just praise and be thankful.
He who began a good work, is faithful to complete it...
You CAN....You WILL ...You MUST have FAITH!

I WRITE BECAUSE

I write because that is the gift within me,
Expressing my inner being.
As Christ intended it to be,
Each one of us has a gifting.

I write to encourage and uplift,
Loved ones and friends around me.
That despite life's bitter and the sweet,
In writing it gives sweet release!

I write because the joy God gives,
His awesome love, the inner peace.
Still waters they say oft runs deep,
But He supplies our every need!

I write when tears of laughter flows,
When storms arise and fires glow.
I write for God has given me ,
HIS peace, His joy and endless love.

I write, I live and breathe poetry,
And love to compose most joyfully.
Touching the hearts of other to see,
God's peace and love from me!

MEN OF GOD ARISE

Men of God arise for faithful is the Lord,
Arise and shout the battle cry;
Be prepared to yield yourself to His will,
Fathers, men know God abides with you still!

It's now time to take up the mantle,
That the Lord has laid upon you.
Being priest within your household,
Leading with dignity and strength, upholding.

The foundation of prayer within the home to keep,
Your loved ones to always uphold.
To teach, as the Saviours face you seek,
Don't let the adversary dare try to come in.

Pleading the blood of Jesus over your family,
Let the Holy Spirit saturate you wholeheartedly.
Don't let negative thoughts and actions permeate your life,
But ask the Lord for direction within your every deed and action.

Let not pride, anger, envy, jealousy dominate your thinking,
But let the Holy Spirit renew your every being.
Let not your heart be troubled you have the strength within,
The power to overcome with Christ, the victory you'll win!

God He knows your daily struggles,
The temptations and troubles you may sometimes face.
But be not ashamed cry out to God,
For His eternal love and awesome grace.

Which will keep your foot from slipping,
When sometimes upon this road of life you tread.
Because fatherhood is not just for a day,
No....it is a lifelong sacrifice instead.

But.... God's word declares He knew you,
From in your mother's womb you were formed.
Therefore your footsteps have been ordered,
From before time, remember.....HE IS the Lord.

From the dust He breathed life into you, you became a living soul,
To always show forth your heavenly father's praising pursuing to be whole.
Through tears, laughter and stormy weather,
The Lord will always be your armour bearer.

Look also to your household and family,
Who love and honour you in their entirety.
Seeing in you the man that you must be,
To help lead them on the right road to eternity.

So love, nurture, be patient and kind,
For in doing you'll find peace of mind.
But also you'll feel their prayers abound,
When sometimes you're stood on shaky ground.

Men you must have vision of where you're going,
Tell me ....can the blind lead the blind? Greatness needs to flow.
You must seek God's will, as you lay hold of your eternal hope,
Which lays within Christ Jesus only, the Saviour of mankind?

So let His Holy Spirit control your very life,
His peace will keep you standing in the bitter days of strife!
Learn to love with meekness, gentleness and kindness,
Strength and honour to behold, the Father's love will always behold.

So yes you can cry tears unto Him, it does not mean your weak,
For humility He'll honour as you lay your troubles at His feet.
He'll restore you an empower you to go forward for His kingdom,
Tearing down the adversaries strongholds taking back what he has stolen.

Standing tall in the power of the Lord,
For God says you are the head and not the tail!
Keep your mind renewed always on the Father's love,
As your foes are vanquished by the power of His blood.

So yes you can arise with strength, the Holy Spirit as your armour,
Your feet shed with the word of God, sharper than a two edged sword.
So father's men of God arise, shine for the Lord,
Blinding the adversary with His might, serving God in one accord.

As you become men committed to His call,
Trust in the LORD you may falter, fail sometimes.
But.... in God your standing tall!

1 Corinthians 10 v 13

SAINTS BEWARE

Saints beware as you smile and say welcome,
Into the sanctuary you greet.
A person from off the street,
God's face to introduce to.

They smile, you laugh,
You're taken in, amidst the slanted grin.
Deception is their master plan,
While on the solid rock you stand.

If you loved me you would...
What lose my salvation over you!
Excuse me, but God has the key,
To my life, you'll only bring pain and strife.

Suited and booted, the flattery rolls,
From the tongue, a devil in disguise.
To think to wreck the heart,
Setting me apart from the Father.

Slick as oil, sweet as a nut,
My heart you separately try to crack.
To break my mentality.....wait,
Or is it to test my sanity?

Yet upon the word of God I'll stand,
Seeing right through your masquerade.
In time, so I do not degrade,
Disgrace, disappoint myself or you Lord.

So look you must look past the outward flesh,
Discern the inner man.
Do not be taken in by flattery,
But let the spirit lead you!

'Let no one deceive you with empty words, for because of these things the wrath of God comes upon the sons of disobedience' – Ephesians 5 v 6 KJV

WHO CAN FATHOM GOD'S WAYS

Who can fathom the very nature of God?
Who made man a little lower than the angels.
He who breathed life into mankind,
Whose divinity surpasses human understanding!

Do we mere mortal men think we are above?
The very heart created in order to love.
Our fellow man irrespective of race,
For God He knows what lies beneath.

Those whose minds and hearts deceive,
While masquerading as a child of His.
As sin lies open and they lie,
Devious spirits, to which some align with.

What is man that He is mindful of us?
When created from dust we were made.
To give Him praise and glory,
Not to pervert His name.

We who say we wear His name,
Must walk upright in order to attain.
Eternal life with Him should be our gain,
Not spoils on earths which cause disdain.

We say we seek to know His glory,
While portraying a very worldly story!
Man cannot serve God and the world,
He'll lose His inheritance and rich reward.

Living life with the God of our salvation,
This is the purpose of our creation.
When we think we are far above His ways,
He rebukes, renews us when we stray!

Who are we to possibly concede we know more?
Of what Our Heavenly Father has in store.
Windows of heaven I need to see,
Partaking with my awesome majesty!

"For who hath known the mind of the Lord? Or who hath been his counsellor? Or who hath first given to him, and it shall be recompensed unto him again? For of him and through him, and to him, are all things; to whom be glory for ever. Amen" Romans 11 v 34-36 KJV

WHERE ARE YOU GOING?

Where will be your resting place?
In the pit of Heaven or hell.
Where are you planting your footsteps?
On the road to life or destruction?
Narrow is the road, straight is the way,
If onto God you wish to remain.
Eternal life to be your reward,
Or a living hell in darkness.
No way out regardless of,
The good life you say on earth you lived.
But did not give wholeheartedly to Him.
He will repay your ignorance,
As you about your life go.
The Saviour you don't want to know.

So where are you going?
You think you can just live your life,
In all your pride and obstinacy.
Why not accept the living word.
In order not to make hell your home,
But worship God in all His Majesty.
A crown of life to wear in eternity.
Hope in Christ is your reality.
Do you know where you're going?
I do because in Him I'm living,
Pursuing and seeking after Him.
My God who vanquished me from sin,
In order to receive my reward,
A crown of life, rather than a sword of death.

I'm on the road, pathways leading to Heaven,
When losing my way God gives direction.
In order for me to reach my final destiny.
He who redeems me enables me to continue,
In praying and praising as I pursue.
Travelling onto His Heavenly Kingdom,
Arriving to my final destination.
BUT....what about you,
Where are you going?

GIVE IT TO JESUS

Why do you carry that heavy load?
Along your journey of life's busy road.
You think you can manage it all on your own,
Why don't you …give it to JESUS?

Why don't you seem to smile anymore?
In its place is heartache, pain, misery galore.
You think no one cares about your soul,
Why not just …give it to JESUS?

Life has it's little up's and downs,
It is not always smiles, sometime you'll frown.
But you must believe you won't always be down.
Why don't you…give it to JESUS?

Give it to JESUS I hear you say,
Why do you care about my day?
Burdens He can easily lift them away
You must just… give it all to JESUS!

Psalm 55: 22 KJV "Cast thy burden upon the LORD, and he shall sustain thee; he shall never suffer the righteous to be moved".

HE'S COMING BACK AGAIN

Triumphantly up from the grave He rose,
Shackles of sins bondage he broke.
Ascending unto heaven from the cross,
My transgressions purchased by His blood.

Know this, He's promised to return,
Breaking through the clouds victoriously.
With an army of angels ready,
To judge the world for its enmity.

Against Him and the earth He created,
They have destroyed and desecrated.
Lawless hearts against Him live,
Abounding in there polluted souls.

Of contaminated lives in sin,
Their very souls He's tried to win.
When He comes back to judge creation,
Our hearts in Him must be unearthed.

Only souled out to Christ the King,
A speck of sin not reigning in,
This body He created here on earth,
To give glory and not be a curse.

But a living sacrifice to Him,
Our Saviour and omnipresent king.
When you come back and return,
I know I must be ready waiting.

The rapture to partake in,
Ascending up with you on high,
Riding high through clouds and skies,
I know you're coming back again.

Your word declares the skies will break,
As you in glorious light awake.
The whole earth to see your power,
Trumpets ablaze in that great hour.

"Saying with a loud voice, 'Fear God and give glory to Him, for the hour of His judgment has come; and worship Him who hath made heaven and earth, the sea and springs of water"
Revelations 14 v 7

www.ingramcontent.com/pod-product-compliance
Lightning Source LLC
Chambersburg PA
CBHW070615010526
44118CB00012B/1519